Celebration The Birthday of

Guests

Guests

Guests

Guests

Guests

Guests

Guests

Guests

Guests

 Guests

Guests

Guests

Guests

 Guests

Guests

Guests

Guests

Guests

#

Guests

Guests

Guests

Guests

Guests

 Guests

Guests

 Guests

Guests

Guests

Gift Log

Gift Log

Gift Log

Gift Log

Gift Log

# Gift Log

Gift Log

Gift Log

Gift Log

 Gift Log

Gift Log

Made in the USA
Monee, IL
27 January 2020